D0769118

Robert Goddard

Rocket Pioneer

Kaye Patchett

BLACKBIRCH PRESS

An imprint of Thomson Gale, a part of The Thomson Corporation

THOMSON

™

GALE

Detroit • New York • San Francisco • San Diego • New Haven, Conn.
Waterville, Maine • London • Munich

For more information, contact
Blackbirch Press
27500 Drake Rd.
Farmington Hills, MI 48331-3535
Or you can visit our Internet site at http://www.gale.com

LIBRARY OF CONGRESS CATALOGING-IN-PUBLICATION DATA

Patchett, Kaye.
  Robert Goddard / by Kaye Patchett.
    p. cm. — (Giants of science)
  ISBN 1-56711-888-7 (hardcover : alk. paper)
  1. Goddard, Robert Hutchings, 1882-1945—Juvenile literature. 2. Rocketry—United States—Biography—Juvenile literature. I. Title. II. Series.

  TL781.85.G6P38 2004
  29.4'092—dc22   2004018815

CONTENTS

A Fiery Launch

Sirens screamed. A police car and two ambulances dashed through the Massachusetts countryside. A line of cars followed. It was July 17, 1929. Neighbors had reported a plane crash at Effie Ward's farm in Auburn. They had seen a fiery trail in the sky, followed by an explosion.

Unaware of approaching trouble, the thin, balding figure of Robert Hutchings Goddard stooped to inspect the remains of his experimental rocket. The press had laughed at Goddard's experiments with high altitude rockets in 1920, after he had published a scientific report of his work. The shy, sensitive physics professor from Clark University wanted no more publicity. He asked only to be left alone.

Goddard smiled at his four assistants. Today's launch at his relative's farm had been most satisfactory. The 11.5-foot (3.5-meter), 35-pound (15.9-kilogram) rocket had carried a thermometer and a barometer, as well as a camera to photograph the temperature and air pressure readings when the rocket's built-in parachute released at the highest point of the flight. It was the first rocket ever to carry a payload of instruments.

The rocket had risen with a roar and a bright white flame. After eighty feet (twenty four meters) it turned to the right, rose ten feet (three meters) higher and then plummeted to earth. The parachute that should have carried the rocket gently down to earth had failed to open. The gasoline tank exploded, but most of the instruments and scattered rocket parts were undamaged.

Despite the problems with the launch, Goddard was pleased. Three years earlier he had launched the world's first liquid fueled rocket. The newest model had flown twice as high as the earlier one. His immediate goal was to send up instruments to study the atmosphere at altitudes higher than a balloon could reach. He did not tell even his assistants his dream that his rockets might one day escape the pull of Earth's gravity and fly into space.

Robert Hutchings Goddard is known as the father of modern rocketry.

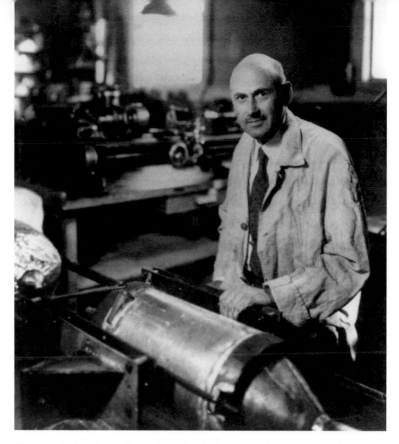

Goddard developed many patents for rocket components. Here he stands next to one of his early rockets.

When the emergency vehicles raced into the farmyard, two policemen hurried toward Goddard. The professor greeted them courteously. It was only a little experiment with a rocket, he explained. He would be grateful if they could keep the matter quiet. One officer shook his head regretfully, and pointed. Two reporters had hurried to examine the blackened rocks beneath the launch tower. The newsmen bombarded Goddard with questions. The next day, a *Worcester Evening Post* headline screamed: "TERRIFIC EXPLOSION AS PROF. GODDARD OF CLARK SHOOTS HIS MOON ROCKET."[1] Goddard was in the news again.

A True Pioneer

Robert Hutchings Goddard is recognized as the father of American rocketry. His pioneering research produced numerous "firsts." Goddard was the first American to work out and publish the mathematical theory of rocket propulsion. He was the first person to prove that a rocket would provide thrust in a vacuum, and he designed and launched the world's first liquid fueled rocket. He was also the first person ever to launch a rocket that exceeded the speed of sound. Goddard developed and patented a host of rocket components, from a gyroscopic stabilizing device to a "curtain cooling" system to prevent the combustion chamber from burning through. His patents were used on all later rockets, including the Apollo spacecraft that took the first humans to the moon.

"The earliest interest in mechanical things appears to have been on a trip to Boston when I was a few months old, and when, I am told, I spent most of the time studying the bell-cord system at the top of the [train] car."

ROBERT GODDARD

Goddard was granted a total of 214 patents, many of them after his death from throat cancer in 1945.

A Curious Youngster

Bob Goddard was born at his grandmother's house at Maple Hill, Worcester, Massachusetts, on October 5, 1882. His father Nahum worked for a firm that made machine knives. When Nahum had married his boss's daughter, Fannie Louise Hoyt, her father had disapproved, but Nahum's mother, Mary Pease Upham Goddard, had welcomed Fannie into her home. When Bob was a year old, the little family moved to Roxbury, a suburb of Boston about forty miles away, where Nahum worked at the knife factory. He later bought the factory and introduced his own ideas. He invented a knife to cut rabbit skins, and a flux—a substance used to purify metals to be welded together—called the Goddard Welder.

Young Bob shared his father's fascination for inventions. As Bob grew up, he experimented with kites, designed waterwheels for a frog hatchery he planned to build someday, and sent off to scientific suppliers for devices that interested him. Nahum and Fannie encouraged Bob's curiosity. They gave him a telescope and a microscope. When street lights first came to Boston, Nahum had electric lights installed in the family home. Together, he and Bob read about Alexander Graham Bell's "talking wires," and the Goddards were among the first in their neighborhood to get a telephone. They bought a phonograph and a radio. Nahum subscribed to *Scientific American*. Each month, father and son studied its articles and eagerly discussed the latest ideas.

Self-Education

While he was fascinated by scientific facts, Bob's favorite reading was science fiction. He read Jules Verne's 1865 novel *From the Earth to the Moon*, which described a spaceship that was launched to the moon like a bullet from a gigantic cannon. As Bob turned the pages, he made notes. He decided that Verne's theory was flawed. No space crew could survive such a violent explosion or such high acceleration and, he reasoned, friction would cause the spaceship to burn when it shot though Earth's atmosphere. If humans ever reached space, he decided, it would have to be by some entirely different method.

Nahum and Fannie were delighted at Bob's curiosity, but they worried about his health. He caught frequent colds, which often developed into bronchitis and pleurisy (an inflammation of the lungs). He started high school in September 1898, but missed much of the term because of illness.

Since Bob could not attend school regularly, he resolved to learn on his own. Most of the books that he read were about science. One book said that diamonds could be made from intensely heated carbon. Bob decided to investigate. In order to make a hot enough flame to heat the carbon, he would need to burn hydrogen. In his attic laboratory, he thrust a tube that contained hydrogen into the flame of an alcohol lamp. There was a terrific explosion. The family maid screamed that she was killed. Bob's parents convinced her that she was alive and then dusted off the budding scientist. Politely but firmly, they asked Bob to find a new line of research. Diamond manufacture was banned.

The science fiction stories of author H.G. Wells inspired young Bob to think about the problems of space travel.

Back to Maple Hill

Soon the family had more serious worries. Fannie fell ill with tuberculosis, a contagious, often deadly disease caused by a bacterial infection that attacks the lungs. The only known cure was rest and fresh air. Nahum sold his business, and the family prepared to return to Maple Hill and the clean country air.

While his parents made arrangements for the move, Bob occupied himself with his books. One day, he picked up the *Boston Post* and was soon engrossed in a new story by H.G. Wells, which the *Post* was printing in installments. It was called *The War of the Worlds*. The vivid story of Martians invading Earth

> "I was obliged by sickness to leave school for two years. This was not really unfortunate for it gave me time to appreciate some of my advantages and to develop tastes which would have remained necessarily dormant had my school life continued without intermission."
>
> ROBERT GODDARD

came to life in Bob's imagination. He read every installment and bought the novel, which he read and reread throughout his life.

Before the move, Bob fell sick again. Nahum and Fannie withdrew him from school altogether and settled down in the big Worcester farmhouse. Nahum's mother welcomed them back. Known to Bob as "Gram," she loved the boy dearly and took great interest in his studies.

The Cherry Tree

Bob enjoyed living at Maple Hill, but he soon felt tired of staying indoors. On October 19, 1899, the thin seventeen-year-old decided to trim the branches of a tall cherry tree behind the barn. Soon he was perched high among the cherry tree's branches. He sawed off a few dead limbs, then rested his tools on a broken branch and gazed up into the clear blue sky. He imagined a small whirling device that flew up, up, until it disappeared from sight. How glorious it would be, he thought, if he could make a machine that could travel to Mars.

Bob abandoned his pruning and climbed down his ladder in a kind of daze. He wrote later: "I was a different boy when I descended the tree from when I ascended, for existence at last seemed very purposive."[2] Bob noted the date in his diary for the rest of his life. He called it "anniversary day." He had found a mission in life. He wanted to reach the stars.

Newton's Laws

Bob yearned to pursue his vision of space travel, but realized that he knew little about the forces that govern the way things move. He tried to make models like the one he had imagined in the cherry tree. He used fast-spinning weights in an attempt to launch his models into the air, but they refused to leave the ground. Then he discovered Newton's laws of motion.

The great English scientist Isaac Newton explained in his 1687 book *Principia Mathematica* that three laws regulate how objects move. The first law is that an object at rest will stay still and an object in motion will keep moving unless it is acted upon by another force. The second law explains that force is measured by multiplying the mass of an object, or the amount of substance it contains, by its speed. An increase in force makes an object go faster, and the heavier the object, the more force it needs to make it move. Newton's third law interested Bob especially. It states that for every action there is an equal and opposite reaction. For example, if a person sits in a wheeled chair and throws a heavy rock, the chair would be forced backward as the rock moves forward.

English scientist Sir Isaac Newton described the laws of motion that Goddard knew were key to understanding spaceflight.

Bob was convinced that, if he could learn how to apply them, these three laws held the key to his dream to launch an object into space. He noted in his diary that any advances he might make toward space travel "would be the result of a knowledge of physics and mathematics."[3]

The Hope of Today
In September 1901, Bob enrolled at South High School in Worcester. He rapidly caught up with the work he had missed and was so popular that his classmates elected him class president. His favorite subject was physics. His physics teacher, Calvin H. Andrews, was delighted to have such a keen student, and the two became friends. Bob told Andrews all of his ideas about space travel and the questions he had about it. He

wanted to know how to land on other planets, how to avoid damage from meteorites, and how people could survive during long interplanetary flights. Andrews encouraged his questions but had no solutions. Science had never considered such unlikely ideas.

Bob discussed Jules Verne's cannon-launched spaceship with Andrews and tried to devise some other means of space flight. He knew that when a gun is fired it recoils, or moves backward. If a vehicle could fire countless shots downward, like a gun, the reaction might make it travel upward, he thought. His diary filled with notes and calculations. As he learned more about physics, he realized that many of his early ideas would not work, but as new ideas crowded his mind he continued to scribble and ponder.

Bob graduated in 1904 at the top of his class. In his commencement speech, "On Taking Things for Granted," he talked about inventions that were once considered impossible. He ended: "It has often proved true that the dream of yesterday is the hope of today, and the reality of tomorrow."[4]

An Unusual Student

As Robert Goddard considered his future, he looked at his failed models and his notes about methods of propulsion that his studies had proven wrong. Impulsively, he gathered up all of his notes and burned them in the dining room stove. It was time to forget dreams and study something practical, he told himself.

Gram borrowed money to pay for her grandson's tuition at Worcester Polytechnic Institute, known as Worcester Tech, and Goddard enrolled in 1904. His major was electrical engineering, but scientific invention was never far from his mind. For an English class, he wrote an essay called "Traveling in 1950." In it, he described a train powered by electromagnets that would travel from New York to Boston in ten minutes through a vacuum tube. He reasoned that in a vacuum there would be no friction or air resistance. He wrote another essay about how to use gyroscopes to balance airplanes. His physics professor A. Wilmer Duff told him to send it to *Scientific American*. The magazine published it but rejected as too farfetched another essay he sent them called "On the Possibility of Navigating Interplanetary Space."

Goddard started to scribble notes about space travel again. One of his ideas was for a vehicle that would consist of many guns, one inside another. As each fired, it would drop away to make the vehicle lighter. As the weight decreased, each shot would give more thrust, or pushing force, to the engine. He calculated that the explosives alone to propel such a vehicle would weigh fifty-six tons (fifty-one metric tons). One March day in 1906, he wrote: "Decided today that space navigation is a physical impossibility."[5]

Even so, Goddard continued to theorize. His notes explored how solar and atomic energy could be used as fuel sources, how to take pictures from space, and how a vehicle could use the pull of a planet's own gravity to slow down enough to land on the planet's surface. He knew people would laugh at his ideas, but he wrote in his diary, "The dream would not 'down'."[6]

"My own dream, however, did not look very rosy. I had on hand a set of models which would not work, and a set of suggestions concerning which I had learned enough physics to know that they were erroneous."

ROBERT GODDARD

On June 11, 1908, Goddard graduated from Worcester Polytechnic Institute with a bachelor of science degree—again, at the top of his class. Duff suggested a career in radio engineering, but when Goddard enrolled at Clark University a year later as a physics major, his thoughts were centered not on radio, but on outer space.

Dr. Goddard

Goddard taught at Worcester Tech for one year to earn money for his graduate studies. In his spare time, he scribbled endless math equations. He wanted to calculate how to achieve enough force to propel a vehicle past the pull of Earth's gravity. A vehicle that could carry enough gunpowder to reach space—

13

a distance then believed to be about two hundred miles (322 kilometers)—would be so big and heavy that it would never leave the ground. He wondered what lightweight vehicle could produce enough speed, power, and energy to push itself to such unheard-of heights. On January 24, 1909, he noted down a new idea—rockets.

Rockets work by a reaction process: As the fuel inside burns, high-speed gases are ejected. As Newton's third law shows, the action of the escaping gases causes a reaction that makes the rocket travel forward. The force of the stream of gases is called thrust. Inside the combustion chamber, a tremendous amount of pressure builds up; but less so at the rear of the chamber where the gases escape. The greater force forward pushes on the front wall of the combustion chamber and accelerates the rocket forward—just as an inflated balloon will shoot forward if it is released before its nozzle has been tied.

Goddard was convinced that this law should apply any-where—even in a vacuum. If that was so, a rocket would work even in interplanetary space. He also pondered the question of fuel. He calculated that a combination of liquid hydrogen and liquid oxygen would be the perfect answer. He would need to use liquids, because in their gas forms hydrogen and oxygen would need an impossibly large tank—too large for any rocket to carry—whereas liquids would occupy far less space. Chemicals like oxygen that make fuel burn are called oxidizers. A rocket that traveled through air-less space would have to carry its own oxidizer to burn its fuel. Hydrogen would be the ideal fuel

"It is rather evident that the rocket is the only device which can be used to send apparatus of any delicacy to great heights. . . . Even the balloon is limited in range . . . it does not hope to reach much over 25 miles, beyond which height the type of rocket under discussion must be resorted to."

ROBERT GODDARD

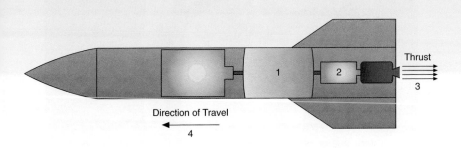

Newton's Principle of Action and Reaction

Thrust

1

2

3

Direction of Travel

4

Newton's Third Law of Motion states that for every action there is an equal and opposite reaction. This is the principle used in powering rockets. Fuel (1) is ignited in combustion chamber (2), creating thrust (3), propelling rocket in opposite direction (4).

because it yielded more heat energy than any other propellant. However, since liquid oxygen was expensive and hard to obtain, and liquid hydrogen completely unobtainable, the idea seemed of no practical use.

In June 1910, Goddard received his master's degree. One year later, on June 15, 1911, he earned his doctorate. Arthur Gordon Webster, head of the physics department, called Goddard's examination "a spectacular performance."[7]

The University of Missouri and Columbia University both offered Goddard well-paid teaching jobs. He turned them down. Teaching would leave him no time for research. Instead, he stayed at Clark for another year as an unpaid honorary fellow in physics. He wanted to continue his research on the movement of electrically charged particles, or ions, inside a vacuum tube. Goddard described this work at a meeting of the American Physical Society. Dean W.F. Magie of Princeton University was impressed by his talk and offered Goddard a research position. Goddard accepted and moved to Princeton, New Jersey, in the fall of 1912.

The Theory of Space Travel

Princeton was old and beautiful, and Goddard settled happily to his research. He developed an instrument, called a continuous tube oscillator, to measure the electric current that flows through a vacuum tube. He later patented the invention, which

Goddard holds the circular vacuum tube that he used in his experiments to prove that rockets would operate in the vacuum of space.

was an early form of radio tube, but did not pursue it further. His cherry tree vision still beckoned.

In the evenings, Goddard worked out his mathematical theory of space travel. In a series of neat tables, equations, and diagrams his calculations showed how much mass a rocket must contain in order to lift one pound (0.45 kilograms) to various altitudes. To overcome the pull of Earth's gravity, he calculated that a rocket would have to travel at twenty-five thousand miles (40,225 kilometers) per hour, and most of its mass would have to consist of propellant. According to Goddard's calculations, 43.5 pounds (19.7 kilograms) of hydrogen and oxygen would propel one pound (0.45 kilograms) into space. However, since liquid hydrogen was unobtainable, Goddard set aside the idea of liquid fuel and decided to experiment instead with smokeless powder—a gunpowder substitute that made almost no smoke.

To minimize the amount of fuel needed, Goddard would have to design a rocket with 50 percent efficiency. That meant that half of the energy given off by its fuel would be transformed into kinetic energy (energy from movement) of the gases and harnessed to power the rocket. He would also have to design a system to feed the fuel gradually into a small combustion chamber so that it would not all burn at once.

Goddard worked far into the nights. During the day, he worked on his experiments in a sealed room filled with sulfuric acid fumes from a hydrogen generator. He coughed frequently. In March 1913, he went home to Worcester for the Easter vacation. His mother rubbed a mixture of snuff and lard on his chest, but this traditional family cough cure failed. Finally, his parents called in a doctor, and then a specialist. The doctors told Goddard he had tuberculosis in both lungs and needed rest and fresh air. Privately, they told Nahum and Fannie that their son had only two weeks to live.

Illness

Goddard ignored much of his doctors' advice; yet, with a nurse to care for him, he slowly improved. Whenever he could, he sneaked his notes from beneath his sickbed pillow and worked on his rocket calculations.

Eventually, Goddard was able to take daily walks. Each day he walked farther. As he roamed the familiar woods and hillsides, he thought about life; it was so fragile and short. Too weak to work full time, he resigned from his job at Princeton. He felt he had no time to lose if he wanted to fulfill his dreams.

Rocket Patents

Goddard's first step was to patent his ideas. He took his rocket notes to a law office that specialized in patents. Charles T. Hawley, the junior partner, helped him to prepare two patent applications. A patent lasted seventeen years. Anyone could purchase a copy of the patent, but no one could use the inventions without Goddard's permission.

In July 1914, Goddard received two patents from the U.S. Patent Office in Washington, D.C. They covered all the basic principles of rocket propulsion. They described solid and liquid fueled rockets, a nozzle and combustion chamber, and different ways of feeding fuels. One patent described a multistage rocket. Each stage would fall away as its fuel was consumed, which would reduce the rocket's weight and allow it to travel farther. The other showed a multiple-charge rocket with a mechanism to feed cartridges of solid fuel one after another, machine-gun fashion, into its combustion chamber. Other diagrams showed how liquid propellants could be fed from tanks into a combustion chamber.

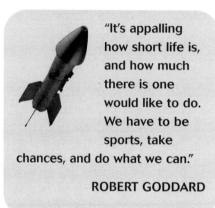

> "It's appalling how short life is, and how much there is one would like to do. We have to be sports, take chances, and do what we can."
>
> **ROBERT GODDARD**

Goddard sent copies of his patents to the U.S. Navy. War had just broken out in Europe, and it seemed that the United States could eventually become involved. Goddard suggested his rockets might be developed as a weapon. The navy wanted to see samples of antiaircraft rocket weapons, but Goddard was not yet well enough to make any kind of rocket. He set the idea aside. By the fall of 1914, he felt better and accepted a part-time job at Clark University to teach a class on electricity and magnetism.

How Do They Work?

As a teacher, Goddard was popular. He loved his subject and his students looked forward to his clear, interesting lectures. Sometimes they applauded or cheered at the end of his classes. Goddard enjoyed their enthusiasm—and, since he taught for only three hours a week, he still had plenty of time for rocket research.

Goddard began to purchase rockets of all kinds and study them methodically. He bought bottle rockets, signal rockets, and the Coston rockets used to fire lifelines. He made a frame to hold the rockets while he measured the amount and speed of their exhaust gases. He found that ships' rockets traveled at about one thousand feet (305 meters) per second. They converted only 2 percent of their fuel energy into thrust, because their widely spread exhaust plumes wasted most of their energy.

To create more pressure, Goddard packed the powder inside his ships' rockets more tightly. He launched the rockets near Coes Pond, outside Worcester. The gases still spread out too widely. To increase their force he designed a narrower nozzle for the gases to escape through. The effect he wanted to achieve was similar to what happens when a gardener uses a hose: With the end of the hose fully open the water flows in a wide, gentle arc; but if the opening is squeezed tighter and the faucet turned up, the result is a straight, powerful and far-reaching blast of water.

At Clark University Goddard shared his enthusiasm for his subject matter with his students.

Goddard tested differently sized nozzles attached to a steel combustion chamber. He discovered that a De Laval nozzle, developed to make steam engines more efficient, worked the best. It narrowed to increase the speed of the gases and then widened again, which allowed the gases to expand and move even faster. On June 16, 1915, he fired a rocket that used the new nozzle and a cartridge-feeding mechanism of his own design. The effect of the nozzle was dramatic. The rocket roared upward at 8,000 feet (2,438 meters) per second and reached an altitude of 486 feet (148 meters).

Success in a Vacuum

Despite this success, Goddard had yet to prove that a rocket could work in a vacuum. Many of his colleagues believed that no reaction could occur without air to push against. To test his theory, Goddard pumped the air out of a long tube in his laboratory. He fired a rocket inside the tube and measured the amount of thrust it produced. The result astonished even the inventor. Not only did the rocket work in a vacuum, but it produced 22

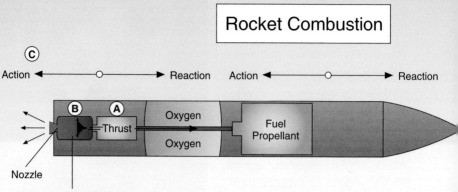

Rocket Combustion

Ⓒ

Action ◄————○————► Reaction   Action ◄————○————► Reaction

Ⓑ Ⓐ

Oxygen

Thrust

Oxygen

Fuel
Propellant

Nozzle

Combustion Chamber

When hot gas under high pressure is produced by the burning of propellant in a combustion chamber (A), the gas will exercise an equal pressure in all directions upon the walls of the chamber. If an opening is made in one side of the chamber the gas will come streaming out at supersonic velocity. At the same time a reaction force will be exerted on the opposite side of the chamber, and it is this reaction force that thrusts the rocket forward.

percent more thrust. The reason, he realized, was that air pressure slowed down the exhaust velocity. That meant that rockets would work better in space than in the earth's atmosphere.

So far Goddard had paid for his experiments out of his own pocket, but he knew he would need substantial funds to develop his ideas further. He decided to write to the Smithsonian Institution in Washington to request support. Established in 1846 for the "increase and diffusion of knowledge,"[8] the Smithsonian displayed collections of historic and scientific interest, published scientific papers, and provided research grants. With his letter, Goddard sent a paper he had written titled "A Method of Reaching Extreme Altitudes." In it he describes his methods and calculations. He explains that his aim is to explore the upper atmosphere with weather-recording instruments that will reach altitudes ten times higher than the twenty miles (thirty-two kilometers) reachable by

Charles D. Walcott of the Smithsonian Institution awarded Goddard his first grant.

balloons. He says that the 63 percent efficiency he had achieved with his rockets is "the highest ever obtained from a heat engine."[9]

Charles D. Walcott, secretary of the Smithsonian, was interested. On January 8, 1917, Goddard was elated to receive a letter from the institution granting him five thousand dollars. Nahum and Fannie shared his delight. Gram, however, his staunch lifelong supporter, had died three months before on October 17, 1916. She had been buried on October 19, the anniversary of Goddard's cherry tree vision. In his diary of the sad day, he noted, "saw cherry tree."[10]

Weapons of War

Now that Goddard had more funds for research, he needed a place where he could work undisturbed. Duff arranged for him to use an isolated building on the grounds of Worcester Tech for a laboratory. Goddard worked to improve his cartridge-feeding mechanism, but his experiments limped along in a series of failures, jammed mechanisms, and unplanned explosions. The device was too complex; something always went wrong.

On April 6, 1917, his research took a new direction. The United States entered World War I, and Goddard wrote the Smithsonian to suggest his invention could be used in the country's defense. The Smithsonian contacted the U.S. Army Signal Corps, who offered Goddard twenty thousand dollars to develop military rockets. Goddard hired a watchman and blanketed his laboratory windows to guard against spies. Some months later the military asked him to

"People are very curious about the work, and indications are that spies are active. Drunken men ring the bell, etc., etc., but disappear quickly when the watchman brings his repeating Winchester shotgun."

REPORT BY C.G. ABBOT ON GODDARD'S WORK FOR U.S. ARMY

The Smithsonian Institution (pictured) contacted the U.S. Army Signal Corps about using Goddard's rockets for national security.

move his operations to a laboratory at Mount Wilson Observatory in Pasadena, California, for added security. Before he moved, Goddard packed all of his notes on space into an envelope and locked them in a friend's safe. He labeled them, "To be opened only by an optimist."[11]

Goddard and his assistants developed two military rockets. One was a long-range rocket, the other was a portable antitank weapon—the earliest version of the bazooka. It had very little recoil and was fired from a shoulder-mounted lightweight launcher. An officer who witnessed some early tests told Goddard, "The stuff you've got there is going to revolutionize warfare."[12] When Goddard and his helper Clarence N. Hickman, a brilliant graduate student, gave a demonstration at Aberdeen Proving Ground in Maryland on November 17, 1918, army officials were so impressed that they promised Goddard more funding to develop a missile to be fired from airplanes. It was not to be. Four days later, the war ended, and weapons research funds were ended too.

Unwelcome Publicity

Goddard returned to Clark University as a senior member of the physics department. In his spare time, he worked on his cartridge-feeding rocket mechanism. On March 28, 1919, his peace was shattered by an exaggerated headline in the *Worcester Evening Gazette*. It announced that Robert H. Goddard had invented a "terrible engine of war," a rocket with an "altitude range of 70 miles."[13] Someone had leaked top-secret information about his war work to the press.

Arthur Gordon Webster, still head of the physics department, urged Goddard to publish his work to counteract the wild rumors. Otherwise, he threatened, he would do it himself. Goddard reluctantly asked the Smithsonian to publish the paper that he had sent them in 1916. He added descriptions of his later experiments and mentioned the possibilities of hydrogen and oxygen as rocket fuels. At the end, he noted that rockets would one day be able to reach the moon. He added that a rocket could explode some photographic flash powder upon landing, so that telescopes on Earth could observe its arrival.

In December 1919, the Smithsonian published 1,750 copies of *A Method of Reaching Extreme Altitudes* and sent a press release to various scientific journals to announce its publication. The result was immediate. Newspapers nationwide and across the world seized on the idea of a moon rocket. They referred to Goddard as Moonie Goddard, and made fun of his ideas. The *Boston American* proclaimed: "Modern Jules Verne Invents Rocket to Reach Moon."[14] A *New York Times* editorial sneered at the idea that Newton's laws of motion could work in space. "Professor Goddard . . . does not know the relation of action to reaction, and of the need to have something better than a vacuum against which to react," scoffed the writer. "He only seems to lack the knowledge ladled out daily in high schools."[15]

The *New York Times* Is Proved Wrong

Always sensitive to the idea that people might ridicule his dreams of space travel, Goddard was angered and mortified by the newspaper stories. He was particularly stung by the *New York Times's* insulting remarks. He often gave demonstrations in

23

Goddard adjusts his portable antitank weapon, an early version of the bazooka.

his classes to show his students how things worked, and one day he showed one of his undergraduate classes an experiment they never forgot. He set up a large glass jar and pumped all the air out of it to create a vacuum. Inside the jar was a revolver attached to a rotating metal post. The gun was set to fire a blank when Goddard applied an electrical charge. He quoted the *New York Times* statement that no reaction was possible in a vacuum—then he fired the pistol. If the article was correct, the pistol would remain still, because it had no air to push against. The class watched in fascinated silence as the gun spun around four times inside the jar. "So much for the *New York Times*,"[16] said Goddard.

"Every vision is a joke until the first man accomplishes it; once realized, it becomes commonplace."

ROBERT H. GODDARD

International Interest

By March 1920, Goddard was inundated with inquiries about his work. Letters came from Japan, the Vatican Observatory, and the German consulate in New York. German scientists seemed especially curious. Because Goddard chose not to publish his ideas about travel to other planets, German publications said he must not understand the potential of rockets.

Now that other people had started to study rockets, Goddard wanted to put his ideas safely on file so that nobody could claim his theories as their own. He sent a report to the Smithsonian that detailed all of his ideas about manned and unmanned rockets, liquid fuels, solar power, space photography, and interplanetary travel. Charles G. Abbot, assistant secretary at the Smithsonian, was politely interested, but he was impatient to see some of the high-altitude flights that Goddard had outlined in his papers. He said he would be more impressed if Goddard could make a rocket that would fly even a few miles.

At Clark University Goddard shows how a rocket could go to the moon.

Naval Rockets

While Goddard wrestled with the design of his multiple-charge rocket, he received a new challenge. The U.S. Navy asked for his help with weapons research. From 1920 to 1923, Goddard was a part-time consultant for a project to develop solid fuel rocket weapons. Life became hectic. His evenings, weekends, and vacations were spent at the Indian Head Powder Factory in Maryland, where the research was located.

> "Although there exists the attitude that 'everything is impossible until it is done,' there is nevertheless widespread interest being taken in the work. To the writer's mind, the whole problem is one of the most fascinating in the field of applied physics that could be imagined."
>
> **ROBERT GODDARD**

Absorbed by his experiments, Goddard sometimes forgot about safety. One day, Lieutenant Commander L.P. Johnson, the officer in charge of research, looked in at Goddard's workshop. He found the professor seated next to a red-hot stove, making pellets of highly explosive smokeless powder. "Beside him was an open twenty-five pound can of powder and he was dusted all over with the stuff,"[17] reported the shaken officer. Goddard promised to be more careful. By 1923, he had developed an antisubmarine depth charge rocket and a rocket that would fire a warhead that could penetrate armor plate.

The Change to Liquid Fuels

As he worked for the navy, Goddard continued to teach his classes and pursue his own experiments. He found that his multiple-charge mechanism to feed solid fuel was too heavy for any but very small rockets. There were other problems, too. Its many complicated parts often jammed or failed, and solid fuels proved too hard to control. Loosely packed powder burned too fast, which could cause a sudden explosion and destroy the rocket. Tightly packed powder burned too slowly and did not provide enough thrust. In January 1921, Goddard abandoned his work on solid fuel rockets. To reach higher altitudes, he needed a lighter rocket with more power, and he needed a liquid propellant, which would burn steadily and smoothly.

According to Goddard's earlier calculations, liquid hydrogen, combined with liquid oxygen to make it burn, would make the perfect rocket fuel. It burned at a much hotter temperature than smokeless powder and would supply far more energy. Since liquid hydrogen was unobtainable, Goddard experimented with propane, alcohol, and other fuels. Finally he decided that gasoline would be the best alternative.

Goddard managed to buy a small quantity of liquid oxygen from a

Goddard stands with his first liquid-fuel rocket. He realized he needed to use liquid fuel to reach higher altitudes.

company called Linde Air Products. Written instructions from the company warned users to keep the chemical away from flame. Goddard did not tell them that he planned to combine it with rocket fuel.

Supplies for the new venture, especially the liquid oxygen, proved to be costly. Goddard's Smithsonian grant had run out, and although a thirty-five-hundred-dollar grant from Clark in 1920 had allowed him to continue his experiments, funds were still limited. Rocket research was an expensive hobby.

Courtship

While Goddard turned his attention from solid to liquid fuels, he also experienced changes in his personal life. On January 29, 1920, his mother died. Despite his sadness, Goddard did not isolate himself in work. His social life had developed over the preceding year. He had several female friends, but he was especially charmed by a young lady named Esther Kisk. She worked

27

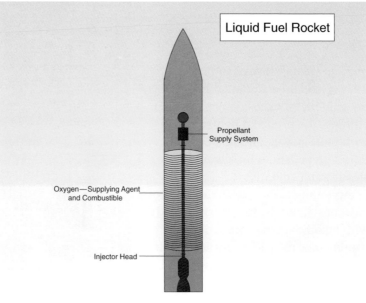

In liquid-propellant rockets the liquid combustibles are contained in tanks and fed into the combustion chamber through an injector head by a propellant supply system.

in the president's office at Clark. They had met in 1919, when she agreed to type Goddard's papers for him. She was seventeen, tall, blonde, and blue-eyed. Goddard was thirty-seven, thin and balding, with warm, brown eyes and a shy smile.

The unlikely pair became friends, and the friendship blossomed into a courtship. Esther's parents thought Goddard too old for their daughter, but they came to like and respect him. When the couple became engaged in 1922, the Kisks did not object.

Early Liquid Fuel Experiments

Goddard's courtship had progressed smoothly, but his pursuit of liquid fueled rocket flight proved more elusive. Liquid oxygen and gasoline were so difficult and dangerous to handle that no one had ever used them for fuel. They exploded if mixed and had to be kept in separate tanks until just before liftoff. Goddard had designed a system of pumps to feed the fuel into a lightweight combustion chamber. One of his assistants, instrument maker Nils Riffolt, said, "Most of our tests ended with something jamming, or sticking, or the chamber burning through. Yet I never saw him discouraged. These were not failures, he usually said, but what he called valuable negative information."[18] Goddard's task was made still more

difficult by the fact that everything had to be made on a miniature scale to conserve liquid oxygen and save money on other materials.

The first tests that Goddard conducted on his rockets were static tests. Instead of firing them into the air, he secured the rockets to a frame and then ignited them so that he could observe how they behaved. This tended to be noisy. People began to wonder about the explosions they heard from the Clark campus. Goddard made Riffolt sign a document that stated he would keep their work secret, but to maintain secrecy they would need a new test site. In the spring of 1922, a distant relative of Goddard's named Effie Ward offered to let him use her farm near Auburn. Aunt Effie took a cheerful interest in Goddard's experiments. When he arrived to test some new apparatus, she would say, "Here comes the rocket man."[19]

The Dawn of the Space Race

Foreign scientists were also keenly interested in Goddard's work. In May 1922, Goddard received a letter from Germany. It was from a Romanian scientist named Hermann Oberth. Like Goddard, Oberth had worked out the mathematics of space travel. He had

Goddard prepares to ignite one of his experimental rockets.

read Goddard's *Extreme Altitudes* paper and was eager to share ideas. Goddard wrote politely that he preferred to work alone. Pioneer work on the mathematics of rocketry had been published in 1903 in Russia by a schoolteacher named Konstantin E. Tsiolkovsky. His paper *Investigating Space with Reaction Devices* was brilliant but purely theoretical. Neither he nor Oberth had ever made a rocket to test their theories. In 1923, Oberth published a paper titled *The Rocket into Interplanetary Space*. It contained many ideas from Goddard's Smithsonian paper.

Romanian scientist Hermann Oberth angered Goddard by publishing a paper that contained many

Angered and disturbed by his belief that his work had been copied, Goddard wrote several papers to show that his work had been done before Oberth's. To the Smithsonian, he wrote: "I am not surprised that Germany has awakened to the . . . development possibilities of the work, and I would not be surprised if it were only a matter of time before the research would become something in the nature of a race."[20]

Overcoming Obstacles

In 1923, Webster died suddenly, and Goddard took his place as head of the Clark physics department. With this promotion came a higher salary, and on June 21, 1924, the thin, gentle physicist married his golden girl, as he called Esther Kisk. Esther knew of her husband's rockets and understood when he worked long hours on his experiments. Sometimes he would lie awake beside her in the old house at Maple Hill as he tried to "dope out", as he put it, the latest problems with his new rocket.

To replace the heavy, unreliable fuel pumps, Goddard decided to use pressurized gas to force the gasoline and liquid oxygen into the combustion chamber. Other problems still had to be overcome as well. The rocket's pipes and valves had to be made stronger to resist extremes of temperature. Gasoline burned at nearly 6,000 degrees Fahrenheit (3,315 degrees Celsius) when combined with oxygen. In contrast, the liquid oxygen had to be kept at -297 degrees Fahrenheit (-183 degrees Celsius) until the fuel was ignited, and it tended to form ice and clog the fuel lines.

To make a combustion chamber that would be lightweight but strong enough to withstand intense temperatures, Goddard finally settled on duralumin; a thin, light metal made from copper, magnesium, aluminum, and manganese. By the end of 1925, after five years' hard work, the liquid fuel rocket was almost ready to launch.

> "Bob Goddard was the most stubborn fellow I ever knew. Once I asked him about his moon rocket. 'Asa,' he told me, 'all I'm trying to do is get this thing off the ground!'"
>
> ASA WARD, AUNT EFFIE'S NEPHEW

A Historic Launch

On March 16, 1926, Goddard picked up his new assistant Henry Sachs and drove through the snowy countryside to the launch site. The ten-foot (3-meter) rocket they erected in a launching frame beside Aunt Effie's cabbage patch was a strange sight. With no outer casing, it had a skeletal look with all of its inside parts open to view. At the top of the rocket was the motor, or propulsion part of the rocket, made up of the combustion chamber and its casing, together with the nozzle and igniter. Long thin fuel lines connected the motor to liquid oxygen and gasoline tanks positioned at the bottom.

At around noon, Esther drove up with Percy Roope, an assistant physics professor at Clark. She had brought a brand-new movie camera to capture the historic launch on film. The spindly, elegant rocket stood ready. A separate cylinder of oxygen gas was connected to the rocket by a garden hose. It would be used to pump oxygen into the system before liftoff, thereby forcing the propellant into the combustion chamber. Once enough pressure had been created, the fuel would continue to feed steadily.

Goddard prepares to launch the world's first liquid-fuel rocket.

At a sign from Goddard, Sachs lifted a blowtorch and heated the igniter—a pipe full of match heads and black powder (a kind of gunpowder) which would catch fire when heated and ignite the fuel. Black smoke billowed out. Quickly, Sachs lit an alcohol stove under the motor to heat the liquid oxygen so it would begin to turn to gas and combine with the fuel. Goddard hurried to the oxygen cylinder and began to pump, which pushed the gasoline and liquid oxygen into the combustion chamber. The fuel ignited with a roar. For ninety seconds, nothing seemed to happen while the rocket built up enough thrust to lift its own weight. Then Goddard released the pressure hose, and he and his men ran behind a sheet-iron barricade.

There was a sharp pop, then a white blast of vapor and flame. With a steady roar, the world's first liquid fueled rocket rose slowly. It gathered speed, shot up 41 feet (12.5 meters) then curved left and crashed into the ice and snow among Aunt Effie's cabbages 184 feet (56 meters) away. It had flown for two and a half seconds.

Esther's camera ran out of film before the rocket lifted off; but Goddard recorded in his diary: "It looked almost magical as it rose. . . . Esther said that it looked like a fairy or an esthetic dancer as it started off."[21] Goddard knew that he had made history. He noted, "As a first flight, it compared favorably with the Wrights' first airplane flight . . . and the event . . . was just as significant."[22]

A "Big Sitter"

Goddard had-proved that liquid fueled rockets could fly, but without more money his experiments would soon be at a standstill. Abbot arranged for a grant of twenty-five hundred dollars from a private foundation; then, in July 1926, the Smithsonian approved a further sixty-five hundred dollars. Goddard immediately set to work to develop a rocket twenty times larger than his first model.

The big rocket proved to be nothing but trouble. It burned more fuel than the smaller rocket and generated much more heat. At each test, the combustion chamber burned through. The rocket never left the ground. In September 1927, Goddard decided the big rocket was a failure. Esther said, "Instead of a little flier, he had built a big sitter."[23]

"He chose a field for his particular search for truth, and devoted his life unremittingly and joyfully to bringing his dream through hope into shining reality."

ESTHER GODDARD

Goddard's next rocket was only four times bigger than his first. He had moved the motor to the base of the rocket and improved the fuel-feeding system, but to his frustration the combustion chamber still burned through. After many patient experiments Goddard found a solution. He invented a device to cool the inner surface of the combustion

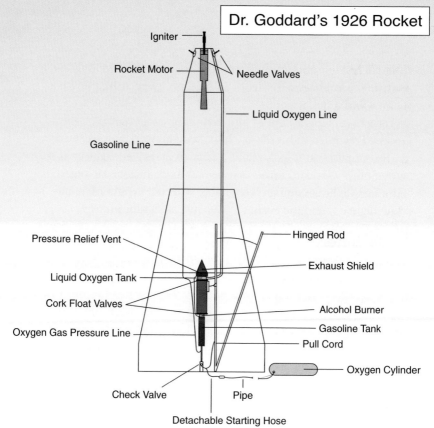

Dr. Goddard's 1926 Rocket

Igniter

Rocket Motor

Needle Valves

Liquid Oxygen Line

Gasoline Line

Pressure Relief Vent

Hinged Rod

Exhaust Shield

Liquid Oxygen Tank

Cork Float Valves

Alcohol Burner

Oxygen Gas Pressure Line

Gasoline Tank

Pull Cord

Oxygen Cylinder

Check Valve

Pipe

Detachable Starting Hose

chamber with a curtain of liquid oxygen. The process was
similar to what happens when a person licks a finger and
then briefly touches it to a hot iron; the finger is protected by
the layer of moisture and will not be burned.

Curtain cooling for rocket engines was one of Goddard's clever-
est inventions, but at first it often malfunctioned. Unless the entire
surface of the chamber was covered with the spray of coolant,
some portion of the wall still burned through. After each failure,
Goddard went calmly back to work to "dope out" the problem.
Esther was concerned by the immense difficulty of his research. "If
it were easy, someone would have done it long ago,"[24] he told her.

It had been a difficult period for Goddard. At seventy
Nahum, who had been a friend to his son as well as a father, lay
dying of throat cancer. Before his death on September 15, 1928,
he asked for Esther. He was too weak to talk, but she understood that he wanted her to take care of his son.

"Nell" Makes Headlines

Esther helped Goddard through his loss and encouraged him as he returned to work on the complexities of his new rocket. The rocket was 11.5 feet (3.5 meters) long, 26 inches (66 centimeters) wide, and weighed 35 pounds (15.9 kilograms) without fuel. It would carry a payload of meteorological instruments to measure air pressure and temperature, and a camera to photograph their readings. An attempted launch on May 17, 1929, failed when the nozzle burned through, but on July 17 Goddard and his crew were ready to try again.

Joining his helpers from the 1926 launch were Esther's machinist brother, Albert Kisk, and Clark graduate student Lawrence Mansur. This time, to Goddard's delight, the rocket flew twice as high. It cleared the 60-foot (18.3-meter) launch tower and rose 30 more feet (9.1 meters). It crashed to the ground 171 feet (52.1 meters) away, and Goddard and his crew hurried to inspect it. The parachute had jammed, but the camera and barometer still worked.

The flight had been a success, but a noisy one. The rocket's loud scream and fiery trail attracted a string of emergency vehicles and reporters to the scene before Goddard and his crew could pack their equipment and beat a retreat.

Secrecy was impossible. The reporters had recognized Goddard as the "moon man." Although Goddard insisted, "There was no attempt to reach the moon, or anything of such a spectacular nature,"[25] the newspaper reports next day were exaggerated and

Goddard poses behind a Nell. His rocketry work attracted the attention of newspaper reporters.

Goddard moved his rocket tests to Camp Devens after a Massachusetts fire marshal banned further testing due to the fire risk.

sensational. Annoyed by the wild stories of a moon rocket, Mansur quoted from an old melodrama about a mistreated heroine: "They ain't done right by our Nell."[26] "Nell" became the nickname for all of Goddard's rockets from that day onward.

A Setback and a Surprise

After the launch, the local fire marshal banned Goddard from further rocket tests in Massachusetts. He said they were a dangerous fire risk. With Abbot's help, Goddard arranged to use Camp Devens, a nearby military range. As federal property it was not included in the state's ban on rocket tests.

The new site was not a success. Its roads were so rutted that Goddard's rockets were usually shaken and damaged by the time he had hauled them twenty-five miles from his Clark workshop. Goddard was frustrated over the delays as one component after another had to be repaired. He wrote to Abbot: "The rocket developments being made in Germany, apparently very substantially supported, make me impatient when things do not move as fast as possible."[27]

German rocket research had indeed moved quickly. In 1927, the Germans had formed the *Verein für Raumschiffarht* (VfR), or Rocket Society. Its eight hundred members included Oberth and scientist Wernher von Braun. Unlike Goddard, VfR members worked in teams and sought publicity.

Wernher von Braun (right) and Oberth attend a 1963 meeting. The two worked together beginning in 1927 as part of the German rocket society VfR.

The time Goddard could devote to his own rocket work was limited. He had a department to run and classes to teach. One gloomy afternoon in November 1929 he sat in his office after class. The phone rang, and he reached to answer it. The caller was Charles Lindbergh. Known as the Lone Eagle, the world-famous flier had made worldwide headlines in 1927 when he flew solo from New York to Paris across the Atlantic Ocean. He told the astonished professor that he had read the newspaper stories about his rockets with great interest. He asked if he could come to visit the next day. Goddard managed to assure him he would be delighted.

Lindbergh Is Interested

Goddard and Lindbergh liked each other at once. The professor told Lindbergh more about his work and showed him movies of his rocket tests. Lindbergh said he believed it was time for aeronautics to go beyond aircraft with propellers; to fly higher, planes would have to use rockets. Now, as he heard what Goddard had already achieved, the young flier was filled with excitement.

"What would help you most in carrying out your experiments?"[28] Lindbergh asked. Goddard replied without hesitation. His dream was to have enough time and money to devote all of his time to rocket research. Pressed to name a figure, he said

"In the fall of 1929 Colonel Charles A. Lindbergh became interested. . . . I flew back from Wilmington to New York with him in his two-seater plane, he taking me up to 8,000 feet, and down to within 50 feet of the tops of the pine trees, the latter proving a good test of my nerves."

ROBERT GODDARD

that a grant of twenty-five thousand dollars a year for four years would provide everything necessary, from assistants' salaries to materials and transportation to a new research site.

Lindbergh wrote later that if Goddard could get the funds he dreamed of, "he felt he could accomplish within forty-eight months what might otherwise take a lifetime."[29] He assured Goddard he would do everything in his power to help him.

Fund-Raising

Lindbergh arranged a conference with the advisory committee of the Carnegie Institution of Washington. The assembled scientists were impressed by Goddard's description of his work. After the meeting, the committee awarded Goddard a grant of five thousand dollars, and technology institutes nationwide began to ask him to lecture about his work. The dreamer from Massachusetts had come a long way. He had earned the respect of his colleagues as a pioneer in a new field, but the vast funds he needed to take his work further were still beyond his grasp.

By May 1930, Goddard had lost touch with Lindbergh, but the flier had not forgotten his promise. Lindbergh went to visit wealthy financier Daniel Guggenheim, whose son Harry had been a World War I naval aviator and was a good friend of Lindbergh's. In 1924, the elder Guggenheim had established the Daniel and Florence Guggenheim Foundation to promote charitable causes. In 1926, the family had also founded the Daniel Guggenheim Fund for the Promotion of Aeronautics to support flight-related research.

Lindbergh told Guggenheim about Goddard's work. Guggenheim questioned him closely. Did Lindbergh believe Goddard's rockets had a future? "As far as I can tell, he knows more about rockets than anybody else in this country,"[30] Lindbergh replied. Later, he telephoned Goddard with good news. Guggenheim had promised to grant Goddard one hundred thousand dollars for four years' rocket research.

New Horizons

Jubilantly, Goddard applied for a leave of absence from his job at Clark and began to seek the ideal location for his new venture. His crew shared his excitement. They took apart the launch tower and packed it, along with rocket parts and most of the tools and equipment from the Clark physics shop, into wooden crates ready for transportation.

Wealthy businessman Daniel Guggenheim gave Goddard a large grant for rocket studies.

"When Dr. Robert Goddard first began his monumental work on the development of rockets, about 1909, there was no real technical information anywhere on the subject. In the thirty-five years that followed, he brought a new science and a new branch of engineering into being, launched a new industry, and probably changed the course of human history."

HARRY F. GUGGENHEIM, PRESIDENT, THE DANIEL AND FLORENCE GUGGENHEIM FOUNDATION

Goddard's men work on a rocket tower in Roswell, New Mexico, a place Goddard found ideal because of its isolation.

Goddard examined climate maps of the United States. "Above all," said Goddard, "we wanted ground with a minimum of people and houses on it, where rockets could rise, or crash, or even explode without wear and tear on neighbors' nerves."[31] The best prospect appeared to be Roswell, on a high plateau in the southeast corner of New Mexico. Its dry, clear weather would offer good visibility, and the town was surrounded by miles of hot, dusty, and empty desert. Its dry climate was also beneficial for tuberculosis patients. Esther was worried about her husband's health. She was afraid his tuberculosis, now inactive, might reappear.

Goddard and Esther set off in their red secondhand Packard coupe on July 15, 1930, for the twenty-five-hundred-mile (4,023-kilometer) drive to New Mexico. The familiar fields of New England were soon left behind as they sped through wide Midwestern plains to the brown, silent landscape of the West, sparsely scattered with low thorny trees, cactus, and tumbleweed.

Roswell

Roswell was all Goddard had hoped. A sheep and cattle town with eleven thousand inhabitants, it had a railroad connection that could be used to freight rocket supplies. Roswell was sunny year-round with very little wind. It would be perfect for rocket launches. He and Esther found a large house to rent three miles out of town, called Mescalero Ranch. It stood at the end of a dirt road and was large enough for the Goddards and all their crew.

When his men arrived, Goddard assigned them to build a machine shop while he located a suitable launch site. Oscar White, a local rancher, offered him the use of "a nice little field" that he owned in a place called Eden Valley, ten miles from Mescalero Ranch. Goddard asked if it was large enough. He did not want to attract attention or annoy any neighbors. The site was quite spacious, White assured him: "About 16,000 acres, I reckon."[32]

Full-Scale Rocket Research

The launch tower was erected at its new site, and Goddard made plans to improve his rockets. He wanted to build a lighter, stronger, and more powerful motor and devise a way to steer rockets more accurately so that they would not tilt during flight. Most of all, he wanted to reach higher altitudes. He erected a frame for static tests one hundred feet (30.5 meters) from his new machine shop. Now he could embark on the full-scale rocket program that he had long dreamed of.

On October 29, 1930, Goddard fixed a rocket to his new static frame. Weights held the rocket in place, and instruments would measure the temperature and the amount of thrust from the burning gases. The fuel ignited, but the nozzle jammed. There was a tremendous blast. The gas tank had exploded. It was the first of many failed attempts, but Goddard remained patient. He improved the valve that regulated pressure so that the fuel would burn

"During the fruitful years of full-time experimentation financed by the Guggenheim family, he was an extremely happy man, doing what he most wanted to do, with adequate funds in optimum surroundings."

ESTHER GODDARD

41

Goddard observes a Nell launching in Roswell while standing in the doorway of his control shed.

steadily, and by the end of the year, Little Nell, as they named the new rocket, was ready for a flight test.

On December 22, 1930, Goddard and his crew loaded Nell, carefully wrapped in quilts, onto a trailer. At Eden Valley, they set up the rocket in the old windmill tower they had brought from Massachusetts. This test too was a failure. The rocket caught on the tower and did not lift off.

Little Nell Beats the Record

The next launch was scheduled for December 30. Again the eleven-foot (3.4-meter) rocket was prepared for takeoff. Goddard hoped it would reach greater altitudes than his previous record of ninety feet (27.4 meters).

Nell, a brave red stripe painted down one side, was unloaded and placed in the tower. As Esther stood by with her movie camera, Goddard ran a last check on the equipment. Mansur retreated to a position 3,060 feet (933 meters) away ready to observe the rocket's altitude. Goddard, Esther, and the other crew members took shelter in their control shed. Pressure from the tanks built up, and then Kisk ignited the rocket.

Slowly at first and then with increasing speed, Little Nell moved skyward. Tilted at an angle, the rocket shot up two thousand feet (610 meters) at five hundred miles (805 kilometers) per hour. Then, with a shrill whistle, Nell descended and crashed half a mile away into the desert sand. The parachute that should have slowed down its fall had jammed. Before the pieces had been gathered up, Goddard had already started on plans to redesign the parachute release and improve the steering mechanism.

Interest in Rocketry Grows

While Goddard worked on his latest rocket with his small crew at Roswell, other scientists were becoming involved in the field of rocketry. In 1930, American scientists formed the American Rocket Society. Then, in May 1931, the German rocket society launched its first liquid fueled rocket, funded by fifty thousand dollars from the German government. The rocket, called the Repulsor, reached an altitude of two hundred feet (61 meters). By August 1931, it had achieved thirty-three hundred feet (1,006 meters). Soon afterward the society was disbanded and the German army started a national rocket program directed by von Braun.

Concerned at the news of Germany's progress in rocketry, the American Rocket Society asked Goddard to cooperate with its members on rocket research. Goddard, whom they had made an honorary member of the society, thanked them but said he preferred to work alone. At Lindbergh's suggestion, Goddard again tried to interest the U.S. military in rocket development but met with failure. The greatest war in world history was over, and another seemed unlikely.

The Gyroscopic Stabilizer

Goddard turned his attention away from matters of national interest to focus on more immediate questions. He was very busy working on a new design for the latest version of Nell. To combat the rocket's tendency to tilt in flight, he needed to devise an automatic stabilizer. He had to solve two problems: The rocket must be able to detect a sideways tilt and then correct its own course. As Goddard said, the device had to be "a veritable mechanical brain directing mechanical muscles."[33]

On April 19, 1932, Goddard's new invention, the gyrostabilizer, was ready for its first flight test. Inside the rocket, a gyroscope was set to spin. When the rocket tilted, the gyroscope would lean the opposite way to keep itself vertical. This motion triggered a sensor connected to four movable metal plates, or vanes, at the base of the rocket. Just as a rudder steers a boat when it is turned in the water, the tilted rocket would straighten itself as one pair of vanes was pushed into the stream of exhaust gases.

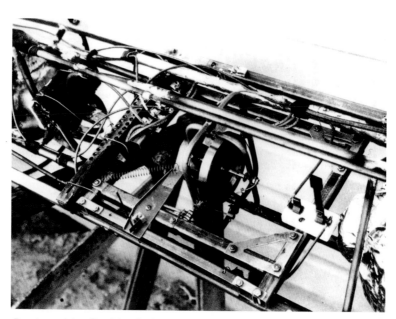

Designed by Goddard, the gyroscopic stabilizer corrected the tilt of a rocket in flight.

The rocket rose straight up for a short distance then crashed heavily to the ground. When Goddard hurried over to inspect the wreckage, he was delighted to find that one of the vanes was warm. The gyrostabilizer had moved it into the exhaust stream. His invention had worked. He decided to make the vanes larger, but in another flight test the following month, the combustion chamber again burned through.

Goodbye to Roswell

Ever since Goddard had started his rocket program at Roswell in 1930, he had been worried that his funding, which was paid to him yearly, might not be renewed. In October 1929, the stock market had crashed, and people all over America had lost their savings because they were invested in companies that had failed. Many rich people had become poor during the Great Depression that followed the crash. Goddard had worried that his research funds from the Guggenheim foundation could also disappear.

Daniel Guggenheim had died in September 1931, but the foundation had continued, headed by Guggenheim's widow Florence and his son Harry. Goddard had been relieved when his second year of funding was approved.

In May 1932, one month after Goddard tested his gyrostabilizer, he traveled to Washington to give his yearly progress report to the Guggenheim advisory committee and to ask for the remaining two years' funds. The committee had bad news for Goddard. As he had feared, the Guggenheim fortune had shrunk due to the Depression. For now, at least, there was no spare money to fund rocket research.

Back at Mescalero Ranch, Goddard had to tell his crew they must leave Roswell and find other jobs. No one wanted to leave, but there was no choice. Goddard had been happy there. Although at times his colds and cough had returned and forced him to stay in bed, he had loved the desert. He had even found time to paint colorful landscapes in his leisure hours. He enjoyed being able to wear old clothes and do the work he loved all day long.

The equipment was repacked and put into storage. The crew left, and it was time for Goddard to join Esther for the long drive back to Massachusetts. He stood for a few moments in the empty machine shed. It was very quiet. He took off his well-worn hat and laid it on a bench. He thought of the formal suits he would again wear as a professor at Clark University. The battered hat belonged with his life at Roswell. "I wonder if I'll ever pick it up again,"[34] he said.

The Resonance Chamber

Goddard refused to be discouraged by the sudden end of his flight tests. If he could not work on large projects, there were still plenty of small components he could develop. Back at Clark University, the only research money he was able to raise was a small $250 grant from

Aviator Charles Lindbergh (second from right) helped Goddard (center) obtain more funding from the Guggenheim Foundation.

Men prepare for a launch at Roswell. Goddard named his new, higher-altitude rockets the "A" series.

the Smithsonian. With this, he hired his brother-in-law Albert Kisk as a part-time machinist, and was soon absorbed in his experiments.

Over the next two years, Goddard improved his gyroscopic stabilizer and curtain cooling system and devised pressure-controlled valves to control the flow of liquid fuels. He took out fourteen patents. One was for an early form of jet engine, which he called a resonance chamber. The device was for use in low-altitude rockets. Instead of having to carry a tank of liquid oxygen, the jet engine would draw in air through a revolving blade called a turbine and compress it. The compressed air would then combine with fuel in the combustion chamber. When the fuel was ignited by a spark, gases would be exhausted from the rear of the engine in a high-speed jet to create forward thrust.

Goddard's new patents attracted widespread interest both at home and abroad. Copies of any patent could be purchased from the U.S. Patent Office, and Goddard's patents—especially those for curtain cooling and gyroscopic steering—were much in demand. German scientists studied Goddard's patents and wrote to him seeking more information, but Goddard politely refused to share any new data.

Funding Resumes

Goddard's work at Clark had attracted international attention, but he longed for the funding that would allow him once more to operate a large-scale rocket program. In the fall of 1933, his patience was rewarded. With Lindbergh's help, he received a twenty-five-hundred-dollar grant from the Florence and Daniel Guggenheim Foundation.

By August 1934, the foundation's finances had recovered enough to grant Goddard another eighteen thousand dollars for a whole year's work. This time he was expected to produce a rocket that would reach high altitudes. Full of confidence, Goddard gathered his crew again and prepared to move back to Roswell.

High Altitudes at Last

Mescalero Ranch was once more full of activity. Equipment was unpacked, and several gigantic crows' nests were removed from the dilapidated launch tower. Goddard, who had again discarded his suits and ties for the more casual clothes he wore at Roswell, picked up his dusty hat from the workbench and put it on. He was back.

A few days later, Lindbergh and his wife Anne flew to the ranch for a visit. Goddard explained to Lindbergh his ideas for a higher-altitude rocket. The new rocket would contain the components he had developed at Clark, with improved stabilizers and a remote control igniter. It would be larger and lighter and would carry more fuel. Eventually, Goddard also planned to develop a lightweight

"How many more years I shall be able to work on the problem, I do not know; I hope, as long as I live. There can be no thought of finishing, for 'aiming at the stars,' both literally and figuratively, is a problem to occupy generations, so that no matter how much progress one makes, there is always the thrill of just beginning."

ROBERT GODDARD

pump to replace the pressure tank that fed fuel into the combustion chamber.

Goddard called his first new rockets the "A" series. They were thirteen to fifteen feet (4 to 4.6 meters) long and weighed up to eighty-five pounds (38.5 kilograms) without fuel. Unlike Goddard's earlier rockets, their pipes and fuel tanks were covered by a metal casing. In the first flight test the combustion chamber burned through. The next test, on March 8, 1935, was a glorious success. Goddard described it as "the best flight we have ever had during the entire research . . . like a meteor passing across the sky."[35] The rocket had reached more than seven hundred miles (1,126 kilometers) per hour—approximately the speed of sound.

Another test on March 28, 1935, proved beyond doubt that the gyroscopic stabilizers worked. During its forty-eight-hundred-foot (1,463-meter) ascent, the rocket twice tilted and then righted itself. On May 31, Nell flew again with a white flame and a roar. This time it reached almost one and a half miles, or seventy-five hundred feet (2,286 meters). A rocket would have to fly five times as far to reach the stratosphere, but it was Goddard's highest flight ever.

Guests and Spies

Elated by his successes, Goddard invited Lindbergh and Harry Guggenheim, president of the Florence and Daniel Guggenheim Foundation, to watch a launch. Lindbergh landed his plane on September 22, 1935, in a swirl of dust. The two men climbed out and Goddard shook their hands with a smile. He had two rockets ready. If one had a problem, the other would be ready to fly in its place.

The next day, the first rocket failed. The igniter burned out before it reached the fuel. The second attempt, after two days of rain, was another failure. The combustion chamber burned through on the launch tower. Goddard was mortified, but his guests encouraged him. They were impressed by his faith in his work and promised to return another time.

Guggenheim and Lindbergh wanted Goddard's progress put on record. They urged him to publish his recent work. Goddard wrote a paper titled "Liquid Propellant Rocket Development" that covered his work from 1930 to 1935. Before it was published on

March 16, 1936, the Smithsonian sent Goddard a copy. The package did not reach him. Goddard's suspicion that it may have been stolen grew when he received other mail that looked as if it had been opened. Some person or foreign power was very interested indeed in the work of the secretive Robert Goddard.

The "L" Series

The mystery of who had tampered with Goddard's mail remained unsolved and he began work on his "L" series of rockets. The new

Goddard inspects an "L" series rocket's parts after a successful high altitude launch in 1937.

rockets were bigger and carried a tank of compressed nitrogen gas that would force the gasoline and liquid oxygen more rapidly into the combustion chamber. Because nitrogen is inert—that is, it does not react with other gases or substances—it would feed the fuel both efficiently and safely. Flight tests began in May 1936 with little success. By January 1937, after several motors had burned through, Goddard realized that his curtain cooling system did not yet work well enough to cool a large combustion chamber. He reduced the diameter of the rocket from eighteen inches (forty-six centimeters) to nine inches (twenty-three centimeters) and decreased its weight from two hundred pounds (ninety-one kilograms) to one-hundred pounds (forty-five kilograms). On March 26, 1937, the new rocket reached the highest altitude that Goddard ever achieved. It flew to between eight and nine thousand feet (2,438 to 2,743 meters) and corrected its flight path perfectly during its twenty-two-second flight.

Encouraged by the spectacular performance of his latest version of Nell, Goddard worked early and late. Esther noticed that he coughed a lot and frequently looked tired. A visit to his doctor confirmed that his tuberculosis had flared up again. Goddard agreed to take a much-needed vacation, and soon he and Esther were headed for California.

During the trip, Goddard called on Robert A. Millikan, president of the California Institute of Technology. Physicists at Cal Tech were also working on rockets and Millikan suggested that Goddard's rocket would progress faster if he shared his work with other scientists. He insisted that rocketry was too big a subject for one man to tackle alone. Goddard refused. He had come too far on his own to let others profit from his ideas.

Germany at War

While the Goddards lived quietly at Mescalero Ranch—or as quietly as the frequent roar of rockets allowed—world events built to a crisis. In the early 1930s, the Nazi party had risen to power in Germany. After World War I, Germany had signed the Treaty of Versailles, under which it promised to reduce military manpower and weapons manufacture. But by 1934 Nazi leader Adolf Hitler had begun to rebuild Germany's military might. Between 1936 and 1939, Lindbergh traveled to Germany several times at the invitation of the German government. The Germans wanted him to see their immense military strength and to spread the message that they would be unbeatable in a war. Lindbergh was not allowed to view the German rocket program—it remained top secret.

After one of these visits Lindbergh persuaded Goddard to ask official U.S. military observers to record the heights his rockets could reach. When the officials arrived at Roswell on June 16, 1938, to witness a launch, a tornado howled through the area, destroyed the tower, and damaged the rocket. On August 9 the officers returned. The repaired rocket shot up in a perfect, vertical flight of 6,565 feet (2,001 meters). Now Goddard's achievements were securely on record.

November 10, 1938, brought news of another disastrous storm—in Massachusetts. A letter from the tenants of Goddard's house at Maple Hill told him that a hurricane had uprooted the old twisted cherry tree that had given him his first vision of space travel. In his diary, Goddard wrote: "Cherry tree down—have to carry on alone."[36]

Lindbergh's fears that German technology had leaped ahead proved well founded. On September 1, 1939, Germany invaded

50

Poland. The Poles' outdated guns were no match for German tanks, and the Germans occupied Poland within weeks. On September 3, Great Britain and France declared war on Germany. The United States was not involved, but President Franklin D. Roosevelt took no chances. He called on top U.S. scientists to form a National Defense Research Committee to research ways to develop new weapons. Because of his reputation for secrecy and his refusal to work with others, Goddard was not invited to participate.

Goddard Is Excluded

Troubled by his exclusion from the committee and eager to help his country, Goddard wrote to the army and the navy to offer his services for rocket weapons research. In May 1940, he was invited to Washington to meet with Army Air Corps representatives. Goddard presented his ideas to a string of officials, who asked him to send a written proposal to further explain his work. The frustrated professor returned to Mescalero Ranch, mailed off the required proposal, and waited.

Months passed, and Goddard began work on an improved rocket: his "P" series. If his rockets were ever to escape the earth's atmosphere they would have to be larger, lighter, and possess more fuel capacity. He abandoned his heavy pressure-feeding equipment and worked to perfect the lightweight fuel pumps that he knew he would need in order to reach extreme high altitudes. Although he was still in poor health, he paid little attention to his cough and hoarse voice and worked as hard as ever. He continued to hope for a contract from the Army Air Corps but so far there was no response to his proposal. It seemed that the technology he had invented would be developed by scientists other than Robert Goddard.

Germany's aggression grew, with attacks on France, Norway, Denmark, and the Netherlands. As Goddard's hope for a military contract dwindled, he focused his attention on his new rocket. His miniature high-pressure pumps forced fuel into the combustion chamber more efficiently than pressure feeding and gave the engine more thrust. However, the mechanism was complicated, and one part or another always failed during flight tests. In May

*Assistants inspect Goddard's last rocket before its launch.
The rocket crashed after a 250-foot flight.*

1941, Goddard launched a twenty-two-foot- (6.7-meter-) long
rocket that weighed five-hundred pounds (226.7 kilogram). It flew
250 feet and then crashed. It was his last launch.

A Naval Contract
The Army Air Corps proved unwilling to fund any more
research, but in the summer of 1941 the navy contacted
Goddard. They wanted him to work on JATOs, or jet-assisted
takeoff devices. With the added speed of a jet engine, airplanes
would be able to take off from the decks of aircraft carriers or
other short runways. When Goddard replied, he enclosed the
design of the jet engine he had patented at Clark. The navy sent
him a contract, and by fall he had hired more assistants and
started tests on jet engines at Mescalero Ranch. By December 3,
1941, static tests showed that the engines worked successfully.
On December 7, Japan attacked the U.S. fleet at Pearl Harbor.
The next day, the United States declared war on Japan. Three
days later, Germany and Italy declared war on the United States.

Under orders from the military, Goddard immediately hired
an armed guard to protect his workshop. In April 1942, he was

told to move his operations to the Naval Engineering
Experiment Station at Annapolis, Maryland. Esther worried
that the damp climate would make her husband's health worse,
but Goddard was delighted at the opportunity to aid the war
effort. He gathered his crew and once more put his rocket
equipment into storage.

JATOs

When the Goddards arrived at Annapolis, a team of scientists
was already at work on JATOs. Goddard's first task was to
develop jet engines to use on the PBY seaplane. His next
assignment was to develop a variable-thrust rocket motor that a
pilot could switch to slow or fast speed as needed. The invention was a success, but the military still showed no interest in
large-scale rocket development.

By 1943, Goddard's throat was so hoarse that he could no longer
speak. When he wanted to give his crew directions he wrote mes-
sages or tapped out words on his desk in Morse code. In August, he
resigned from his job at Clark, long held open for him. Without a
voice he would not be able to teach. The Florence and Daniel
Guggenheim Foundation had promised him more funds, and he
planned to return to Mescalero Ranch when the war was over to
continue his research.

V-1s and V-2s

On June 6, 1944, the Allies invaded France. One week later, a desperate Germany began to fire rocket-powered V-1 bombs at England from the coast of France. The letter "V" stood for *Vergeltungswaffe*, or vengeance weapon. The twenty-five-foot (7.6-meters) V-1 was a winged metal cylinder with a ton of explosives in its nose cone. Powered by a jet engine and steadied by a gyroscope, it glided to a preset target after its engine was shut off. It could travel for one hundred miles (161 kilometers) at speeds up to 450 miles (724 kilometers) per hour. When Goddard read a description of the V-1, he recognized that it was powered by a resonance chamber much like the one he had patented.

"I don't think he ever got over the V-2. He felt the Germans had copied his work and that he could have produced a bigger, better and less expensive rocket, if only the United States had accepted the long-range rocket."

WARTIME COLLEAGUE OF GODDARD'S

About twenty thousand buzz bombs, as the V-1s became known, were fired at English cities. In September 1944, after the Allies had destroyed the V-1 launch sites, the Germans fired their ultimate weapon—the V-2—at Paris and London. More than four thousand of the unstoppable rockets were launched. Twice as large as the V-1, the V-2 could travel twice as far and inflict twice as much damage.

It weighed nine thousand pounds (4,082 kilograms) without fuel, and flew at twenty-six miles (5,792 kilometers) per hour to an altitude of up to sixty miles (109 kilometers). Its thrust was said to be fifty-six thousand pounds (25,225 kilograms). The German rocket program—with billions of Deutschmarks and thousands of workers and top scientists at its disposal—had developed the rockets that Goddard had worked for more than twenty years to produce.

In March 1945, the U.S. army found an unexploded V-2 and shipped it to America for Goddard to inspect. When he

Soldiers in World War II sit on a failed German V-1 bomb, whose rocket design was similar to Goddard's.

dismantled the V-2, Goddard found that it looked familiar. Several of its components—including fuel pumps, gyroscopic stabilizers, and curtain cooling systems—were covered by his patents. The V-2 was made of duralumin and fueled by liquid oxygen and alcohol. Goddard said little as he worked on the giant rocket, but Mansur said later that it was "enough like our Roswell rocket to be its son."[37]

Two months later Hitler died, and Germany surrendered soon afterward. As soon as von Braun, Oberth, and other top German rocket scientists heard of Hitler's death, they surrendered to the Americans. They wanted to continue their research, and realized that the United States could provide the resources that would allow them one day to attain their goal of interplanetary travel. After their surrender, they insisted they had not imitated Goddard's rockets, but had developed a similar design independently.

Death of a Dreamer
In June 1945, Goddard was diagnosed with throat cancer. On July 5, he had surgery to remove his larynx, or voice box, to prevent the spread of his cancer. Weak but undaunted, he wrote notes to thank his doctors for their care and to ask

Hawley, his patent attorney, to finish a patent application he had begun. On August 10, 1945, he died peacefully.

After Goddard's death, Esther began the gigantic task of putting his papers into order. With Hawley's help she filed numerous patents from the vast pile of notes her husband had left behind. As a result, 131 more patents were issued to Robert Goddard.

Goddard's Legacy

After the war ended, the U.S. government started a rocket program with the help of von Braun and other scientists. Many of their rocket components were Goddard's patents, and in 1951 Esther and Guggenheim filed a claim against the government for patent infringement. In June 1960 the recently formed National Aeronautics and Space Administration (NASA) agreed to pay 1 million dollars for the use of more than two hundred of Goddard's patents.

After Goddard's death, honors were heaped upon him for his pioneering work. In 1959, the U.S. Congress voted to honor him with the Congressional gold medal. In July 1960, the American Rocket Society placed a marker at the site of his 1936 liquid fuel rocket launch. On March 16, 1961, the thirty-fifth anniversary of the historic launch, Goddard's friends and colleagues gathered for the dedication of NASA's new Goddard Space Flight Center at Greenbelt, Maryland.

Less than two decades after the death of the dreamer from Massachusetts, space flight moved from the pages of science fiction to become a multimillion-dollar reality.

"Sitting in his home in Worcester, Massachusetts, in 1929, I listened to Robert Goddard outline his ideas for the future development of rockets. . . . Thirty years later, watching a giant rocket rise above the Air Force test base at Cape Canaveral, I wondered whether he was dreaming then or I was dreaming now."

CHARLES A. LINDBERGH

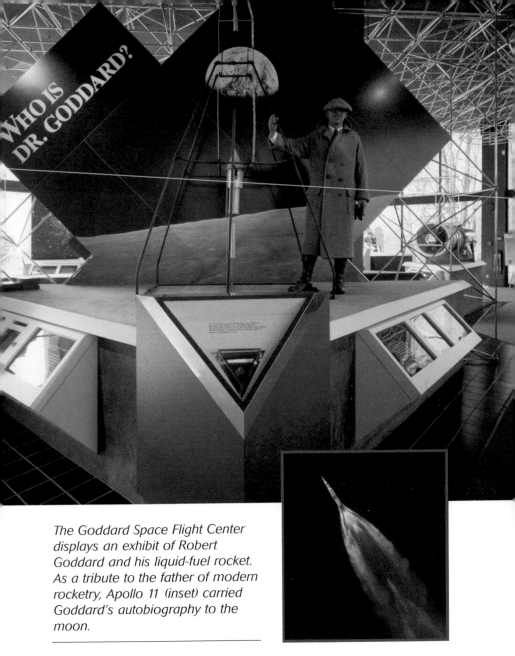

The Goddard Space Flight Center displays an exhibit of Robert Goddard and his liquid-fuel rocket. As a tribute to the father of modern rocketry, Apollo 11 (inset) carried Goddard's autobiography to the moon.

On July 20, 1969, when the United States landed two men on the moon, Goddard's autobiography was carried on board the Apollo 11 space rocket. Three days before, the *New York Times* printed an apology for its 1920 editorial. It said, "It is now definitely established that a rocket can function in a vacuum as well as in an atmosphere. The *Times* regrets the error."[38]

IMPORTANT DATES

1882 October 5   Robert Hutchings Goddard is born in Worcester, Massachusetts.

1899 October 19   Goddard imagines a space vehicle while pruning a cherry tree. The experience moves him to devote his life to space research.

1904   Goddard graduates from South High School in Worcester at age twenty-one.

1908   Goddard earns a BS degree from Worcester Polytechnic Institute.

1910   Goddard earns a master's degree from Clark University in Worcester.

1911   Goddard earns doctorate degree from Clark University.

1912   Goddard is hired at Princeton University as a research instructor in physics. While there, he works out the mathematical theory of rocket propulsion.

1913   Goddard is diagnosed with tuberculosis.

1914   Goddard is hired as a part-time instructor at Clark University. He begins rocket experiments and receives his first two patents, which cover all the basic principles of rocket propulsion.

1915   Goddard becomes an assistant professor at Clark University.

1917   The Smithsonian Institution gives Goddard the first of several grants for high-altitude research.

1918   Goddard works for the U.S. Army. He develops two rocket weapons, one of which is an early form of the bazooka.

1919   The Smithsonian publishes Goddard's paper "A Method of Reaching Extreme Altitudes."

1920 January 13   The *New York Times* publishes an editorial that says Goddard is wrong to believe that a rocket could work in space. Goddard is appointed full professor at Clark.

1923   Goddard becomes head of the physics department at Clark.

1924 June 21   Goddard marries Esther Kisk in Worcester, Massachusetts.

1926 March 16   Goddard launches the world's first liquid propellant rocket at Auburn, Massachusetts.

IMPORTANT DATES

1929	Goddard's launch of his first rocket with a payload of instruments attracts unwelcome publicity. He is banned from flying rockets in Massachusetts and moves his tests to Camp Devens, a military range.
November 23	Goddard meets Charles A. Lindbergh.
1930	Goddard receives a one-hundred-thousand-dollar grant from Daniel Guggenheim for four years' research. He moves to Roswell, New Mexico, to start full-time rocket research.
1932	Goddard invents the gyroscopic stabilizer. He returns to Clark for two years, where he develops various rocket components. He receives fourteen patents, including one for a resonance chamber—an early form of jet engine.
1934	Goddard's Guggenheim funding is restored. He returns to Roswell and begins work on his "A" series rockets.
1935 March 8	One of Goddard's rockets exceeds the speed of sound in a test flight.
1936	The Smithsonian publishes Goddard's paper, "Liquid Propellant Rocket Development."
1939	World War II begins.
1941 May	Goddard launches his last rocket. In summer he receives a contract from the U.S. Navy to develop JATOs.
December 8	The United States enters WWII.
1942	Goddard moves to the Naval Engineering Experiment Station in Annapolis, Maryland, to work on JATOs.
1944	The Germans launch V-1 and V-2 rockets in a last attempt to win the war.
1945	Goddard examines a captured German V-2 rocket. He finds that it contains many components that he invented.
August 10	Goddard dies of throat cancer.

NOTES

1. Quoted in Esther C. Goddard, ed., and G. Edward Pendray, assoc. ed., *The Papers of Robert H. Goddard*, vol. 2:1925–1937. New York: McGraw-Hill, 1970, p. 673.

2. Quoted in Esther C. Goddard, ed., and G. Edward Pendray, assoc. ed., *The Papers of Robert H. Goddard*, vol. 1: 1898–1924. New York: McGraw-Hill, 1970, p. 9.

3. Quoted in Goddard and Pendray, *The Papers of Robert H. Goddard*, vol. 1, p. 10.

4. Quoted in Goddard and Pendray, *The Papers of Robert H. Goddard*, vol. 1, p. 66.

5. Quoted in Goddard and Pendray, *The Papers of Robert H. Goddard*, vol. 1, p. 74.

6. Quoted in Goddard and Pendray, *The Papers of Robert H. Goddard*, vol. 1, p. 11.

7. Quoted in Milton Lehman, *This High Man: The Life of Robert H. Goddard*. New York: Farrar, Straus, 1963, p. 57.

8. Quoted in Smithsonian Institution, "An Unexpected Bequest." www.si.edu/about/history.htm.

9. Quoted in Goddard and Pendray, *The Papers of Robert H. Goddard*, vol. 1, p. 172.

10. Quoted in Goddard and Pendray, *The Papers of Robert H. Goddard*, vol. 1, p. 176.

11. Quoted in Lehman, *This High Man*, p. 91.

12. Quoted in Lehman, *This High Man*, p. 95.

13. Quoted in Goddard and Pendray, *The Papers of Robert H. Goddard*, vol. 1, p. 316.

14. Quoted in Lehman, *This High Man*, p. 104.

15. Quoted in Clark University, Dr. Robert H. Goddard Web Pages. http://libref.clarku.edu/offices/library/archives/GoddardFAQ.htm

16. Quoted in Clark University, Dr. Robert H. Goddard Web Pages.

17. Quoted in Lehman, *This High Man*, p. 122.

18. Quoted in Lehman, *This High Man*, p. 128.

19. Brochure, American Institute of Aeronautics and Astronautics, to commemorate the 75th anniversary of first liquid fueled rocket flight.

20. Quoted in Goddard and Pendray, *The Papers of Robert H. Goddard*, vol. 1, p. 498.

21. Quoted in Goddard and Pendray, *The Papers of Robert H. Goddard*, vol. 2, p. 581.

22. Quoted in Goddard and Pendray, *The Papers of Robert H. Goddard*, vol. 1, p. 30.

23. Quoted in Lehman, *This High Man*, p. 150.

NOTES

24. Quoted in Lehman, *This High Man*, p. 147.

25. Quoted in Goddard and Pendray, *The Papers of Robert H. Goddard*, vol. 2, p. 671.

26. Quoted in Lehman, *This High Man*, p. 156.

27. Quoted in Goddard and Pendray, *The Papers of Robert H. Goddard*, vol. 2, p. 714.

28. Quoted in Lehman, *This High Man*, p. 162.

29. Quoted in Lehman, *This High Man*, p. 162.

30. Quoted in Lehman, *This High Man*, p. 174.

31. Brochure, American Institute of Aeronautics and Astronautics to commemorate the 75th anniversary of first liquid fueled rocket flight.

32. Quoted in Lehman, *This High Man*, p. 182.

33. Quoted in Lehman, *This High Man*, p. 194.

34. Quoted in Lehman, *This High Man*, p. 197.

35. Quoted in Goddard and Pendray, *The Papers of Robert H. Goddard*, vol. 2, p. 908.

36. Quoted in Esther C. Goddard, ed., and G. Edward Pendray, assoc. ed., *The Papers of Robert H. Goddard*, vol. 3: 1938–1945. New York: McGraw-Hill, 1970, p. 1216.

37. Quoted in Lehman, *This High Man*, p. 388.

38. Quoted in Clark University, Dr. Robert H. Goddard Web Pages.

GLOSSARY

black powder: A type of gunpowder that contains potassium nitrate, charcoal, and sulfur.

Earth's atmosphere: The layers of gases that surround Earth. Space begins at an altitude of about 50 to 100 miles (80.5 to 161 kilometers).

gyroscope: A device that consists of a metal wheel that spins rapidly around a spindle inside a circular frame. If its base is rotated, the axis of the wheel will remain upright.

jet engine: A reaction engine that is propelled forward by the hot exhaust gases that are generated when fuel burns.

kinetic energy: The energy present in all moving objects.

mass: The amount of material in a substance or object.

oxidizer: A chemical that combines with fuel to make it burn.

payload: The cargo carried on board a rocket that is not part of the rocket itself, such as scientific instruments or other objects.

recoil: The backward movement of a gun when it is fired.

smokeless powder: An explosive used as a propellant that makes relatively little smoke when exploded.

static test: A way to test the performance of a rocket without launching it. The rocket is secured to a frame so that it cannot lift off. In this way, its exhaust gases can be measured and its engine and other components tested.

stratosphere: The second layer of Earth's atmosphere, extending from approximately seven to thirty miles (eleven to forty-eight kilometers) above Earth's surface.

thrust: The force of a rocket's engine. Thrust is measured by multiplying the mass of ejected gases per second by their speed.

FOR MORE INFORMATION

Books

Suzanne M. Coil, *Robert Hutchings Goddard: Pioneer of Rocketry and Space Flight*. New York: Facts On File, 1992.

Karin Clafford Farley, *Robert H. Goddard*. Englewood Cliffs, NJ: Silver Burdett, 1991.

Milton Lehman, *This High Man: The Life of Robert H. Goddard*. New York: Farrar, Straus, 1963.

Richard Maurer, *Rocket! How a Toy Launched the Space Age*. New York: Crown, 1995.

Tom Streissguth, *Rocket Man: The Story of Robert Goddard*. Minneapolis: Carolrhoda, 1995.

Web Site

The Robert Hutchings Goddard Home Page
(www.clarku.edu/offices/library/archives/Goddard.htm).
Clark University's Robert H. Goddard Library Web site
offers information about Robert Goddard's life, drawings of
many of his rockets, frequently asked questions about
Goddard, and a list of all his papers and articles.

INDEX